OVER

IT

Fear is not an option

Do Not Fear

Be Strong

Reclaim your Power

FEAR IS NOT AN OPTION!!

Acknowledgements

It is so amazing to me how time has gone by but even with time moving Charles Bolar you never did move you stood still and sought God faithfully. I am so grateful, when I felt like I couldn't achieve different goals set before me you encouraged me not to be afraid to obey God and do what he has for me to do. I want to say thank you sweetheart for your love and patience and the role you took in helping me to get this book done.

I want to acknowledge my children and grandchildren for opening my eyes to the importance of overcoming my own fears and issues of rejection and anger. You all are so important to me but remember Christ Jesus is the reason that we can live, love and rejoice. Fear or failure of being rejected by others is not an option. We must become fearless. I love you Alta Mathews, Hannah and Joshua Pugh my three blessed children. I so appreciate my daughter- in- love Shalese Pugh that has stood with this family and has been a great support to me, thank you for your love and prayers.

Now to the editors and those that took out the time to say "don't stop, you can do this" I am grateful to you. I appreciate you Lee Franklin, Talisha Harris thank you for pushing me further in what God has anointed and appointed me do. Can I say no more fear? I am an overcomer through Christ Jesus.

Introduction

Do Not Fear, Be Strong, Fear is not an option!

This book is written with the intent of the reader to regain their strength and peace through daily prayer, reading the word of God and journaling. To rethink our lives, we must speak differently and think differently concerning ourselves. Prayer is essential and filling our spirit with the God is even more essential. We can never overcome the tormenting spirit of fear if we have no knowledge of how God's plan for us to conquer fear, intimidation, depression and a loss of joy.

Our God is the most amazing God when he spoke and said let there be it is being (Genesis 1). The Lord understood everything that would be and would happen in our lives. Jesus knew we would lose love ones, sickness would occur, moments of sudden and unexpected incidents would happen. This is what the word of God says in Ecclesiastes 3:1 To everything there is a season and a time to every purpose under the heaven. There is a time for all things, there is a time for birth and death a time to plant, a time to pluck up that which is planted and a time to heal. Just know this is your time to be healed, be healed of fear and weakness. As you read, pray and write. Each day will bring you to a greater peace and strength. Take time to meditate on the word of God. Give yourself twenty to thirty minutes of quiet time, if you feel like you are too busy and just can't find the time take ten minutes of time and increase it gradually.

We must take our lives back from the snare of the fowler and the actions of the enemy. First thing is being able to give us time to ourselves taking time to bask in the intimate time you have with God.

Fear will make you sometimes afraid even to give yourselves time to focus on you. The phrase what if comes up, what if I miss a call, what if my husband needs me, what if something happens to my children, what if, what if, what if…That fear of losing the place of feeling like you are needed. That dark miserable place of guilt that says if I don't people won't like me and if I do people will talk about me.

We declare strength, joy and victory over your life. As you begin your journey in journaling may the Lord empower you to become completely free of fear and frailty.

Fighting against the spirit of fear

40 days of prayer and affirmations

Often fear will consume a person through traumatic situations such as car accidents, sudden death, physical or verbal abuse, sudden illness, broken marriage, major loss of material goods, loss of jobs, homelessness and many other things can cause fear and a loss of strength.   As you begin day one remember this prayer journal is a daily reminder that despite our issues we do not have to fear and overcoming fear and weakness is like dealing with anything else. You must speak life into a situation that would appear to be hopeless. There is power in your tongue to speak life today we choose life so let's begin.
(Proverbs 18:21)

May this Prayer journal bless you all the days of your life and as you proceed each day in prayer and journaling I speak that every chain be broken off of your life in Jesus Holy name. Here's to Freedom!!!!

Contents

Day 1   My eyes are open to you Lord

Isaiah 51:1 Hearken unto me ye that know righteousness the people in whose heart is my law; fear ye not the reproach of men neither be ye afraid of their reviling's.
Reviling means to insult or criticize.
The Lord is a God that will bring comfort to his people. His desire is for us to be attentive to him. To keep our eyes on him and not on man. Man will fail us and we are not to put our confidence in flesh but rather the Lord our life sustainer.
Focus on Him and trust Him
Today oh God I will hearken unto you not only are my ears open to hear, but my eyes are open to see, reveal unto me that which has been hidden. My soul longs for you, often I have sat still in fear, but I declare that I will be free of fear. For your word is in my heart and daily will I seek after you.

No longer will I read your word and not trust your word. Lord I Believe but help my unbelief. This day is the start of many more wonderful days. Today I make a choice to stand brave and bold. I will rejoice when people insult me rather then run into a dark cave and hide.

I will stand strong in your righteousness and grab hold to the freedom that you have given through salvation. Father, I praise your Holy name and I will forever be grateful of your amazing love that you continually show towards me in Jesus name. Amen

Notes:

Notes:

Day 2 Faint not

Psalms 27:13-14 I had fainted, unless I had believed to see the goodness of the Lord in the land of the living. 14. Wait on the Lord: be of good courage, and he shall strengthen thine heart.

Lord we thank you today for your strength and power. For there have been days when I was truly ready to give up and throw in the towel, but Father I realize I cannot give up for I am determining to see your goodness in the land of the living.

When I feel forsaken you will uphold me, Jesus you truly are my strength and the light of my salvation. You guide me and brighten up those things that could have or would have put me or kept me in a place timidness. I am excited about what you are doing in my life, truly you are my strength and I have nothing to fear.

So today I confess, I am strong in you and will wait and be of good courage because it is only you that has ever daily strengthened my heart. Thank you, Lord, for this day in

Jesus name, Amen

Notes:

Notes:

Day 3   I will trust

Psalms 56:3 What time I am afraid, I will trust in you.

Father I put my trust in you when I feel stressed or I am in distress by cares of sudden issues in my life. I trust you when life seems to be spinning out of control and I feel as though I have lost my direction. I look to you and your guidance, it is a guarantee I will make it if I follow you the good Shepherd.

I realize within an instance when fear tries to consume me I must trust you and know that you will bring me through. I declare that I am coming out of the place of despair and fear. Lord I wait patiently to hear your voice.

Notes:

Notes:

Day 4 Casting

Psalms 55:22 Cast thy burden upon the Lord, and he shall sustain thee: he shall never suffer the righteous to be moved

1 Peter 5:7-10   7. Casting all your care upon him; for he careth for you. 8. Be sober, be vigilant; because your adversary the devil, as a roaring lion, walketh about, seeking whom he may devour: 9. Whom resist steadfast in the faith, knowing that the same afflictions are accomplished in your brethren that are in the world. 10. But the God of all grace, who hath called us unto his eternal glory by Christ Jesus after that ye have suffered a while, make you perfect, establish, strengthen, settle you.

Have you ever wondered why you feel like you are giving everything to God yet there seems to still be a struggle in your life? May I make this suggestion to you it's not that God is not helping you, but it's at that moment you begin to gain strength.

Now you begin to release everything it's then you can walk with a clearer view during your process in this part of your life. Knowing that devil had a plan all along to destroy you. As you go through the process the Lord will mature you, establish you, give you strength and give you peace. Cast your cares begin the process it doesn't complete it.

Look at the word casting it's to throw something, Therefore I will throw not toss because it's a lighter movement but when you throw there must be a push behind what you are doing. So today is when you throw yourself into prayer release all your burdens, those things that weary you, unto the Lord. The Lord never said in this passage that it would be removed what it says is he will sustain you, keep you and the righteous, those that are in right stance with him will not be moved.

In other words, he the Lord will now give you the strength to deal with whatever the issue may be, and you will walk through it all.

God you are the almighty and truly these burdens are more than I can bear. With you Lord I can do this, I am not asking you to just remove these issues but empower me from on high and enable me today to press through this process. Father as I ponder, I know that someone else is burden down and they may not know you like I do. So, God give them strength and help me to be a help to others that we may all come through each day when we face challenges you allow us to see those things that may keep us in a dry place a place of heaviness.

I know that if I cast my cares on you, because you care for me you will give me what I need to move forward.

I am smiling Lord because I am not alone I have someone who care about me and my life. The things I can't speak out loud I can tell you those hidden burdens and pains and as I learn to release them each day I know Lord I will be able reach another person and tell them they can and will make it through.

Thank you for bearing the weight of my troubles and directing my path I graciously receive your grace and love that you have shown towards me In Jesus name, Amen

Notes:

Notes:

Day 5 The Kings table

2 Samuels 4:4 And Jonathan, Saul's son, had a son that was lame of his feet. He was five years old when the tidings came of Saul and Jonathan out of Jezreel, and his nurse took him up, and fled: and it came to pass, as she made haste to flee, that he fell, and became lame. And his name was Mephibosheth.

2 Samuel 9:6 Now when Mephibosheth, the son of Jonathan, the son of Saul, was come unto David, he fell on his face, and did reference. And David said, Mephibosheth. And he answered, Behold thy servant! 7. And David said unto him, Fear not: for I will surely shew thee kindness for Jonathan thy father's sake and will restore thee all the land of Saul thy father; and thou shalt eat bread at my table continually.

In life we have good people that may some way hurt us not by literally dropping us but by dropping us with harsh words, pressures we did not expect to have in our lives, living a lavish lifestyle and going to a place of literally nothing.

Mephibosheth nurse intent was not to hurt him but to help Mephibosheth. She was afraid, her heart was to save him not hurt him. This nurse was running for their lives. Now dropped and placed in Lu-debar the spirit of fear, abandonment, rejection, hurt and sudden lost is developing a child that once sat with his father at the king's table now sit in Lo-debar with little hope.

As he lived in a land of nothing God brought back to King David a vow he made with his friend Jonathan. David found Mephibosheth and once again although Mephibosheth felt as though he was nothing because of life issues that had molded his life he was brought to the King's table there to eat and live forever more.

God wants to bring us to the King's table he is our King and it is he there will prepare a table before us in the presence of our enemy.

Today Lord we think you that although we were dropped and filled with fear as a child. I understand fear begets fear. I come excitedly to the table of the King and I now will sit and sip with you. Your word declares you will never leave me nor forsake me.

As I now look over my life I realize you kept me while I was in the valley. Those that may have brought me to the valley Lord I now realize that they may have been just as troubled as me.

Thank you, Father, for not destroying them but keeping them while they were in the valley as well. I am now free of my past I make a decision now to release my childhood pains, bye physical abuse, so long sexual abuse, see your emotional abuse. No longer do I walk with not forgiving me I choose to love me again because I am lovable, so long emotional abuse.

Now Lord I rejoice that you have brought me out once again to the table of plenty, this table is full of joy, peace, mercy, forgiveness, trust and acceptance.

I declare the Joy of the Lord is my strength and he is my shield and buckler. I declare that I will walk in his goodness and mercy daily for God is my King of Kings and now rest at his table.

In Jesus Name

Notes:

Notes:

Place of fear that had to be broken

My testimony

When I was a little girl I lived with my grandparents and I remember in my early years before the age of 5 or 6 it was a place that was clean, so clean you could eat off the floor. Over the years something changed in my grandmother because of the behavior of my grandfather she became fearful, depressed and her strength was slowly drained out of her.

You see my grandfather was a very strong-willed man, he was quick tempered and full of anger although he may have loved his family he didn't know how to express it nor show it. He was consumed himself by the circumstances of his past. Therefore, his communication was not communication it was yelling and beating. My assumption would be there was indeed a generational curse that trails him.

I remember I was at home with my grandparents and my grandfather was so angry at my grandmother not because my grandmother did anything awful but she simply questioned something that had happen. She realized he was cheating on her but this would not be the last time because it was his lifelong pattern I saw as I grew up.

He beat her, threw dishes and cursed at her as if she had done something wrong by asking him about what she heard. This time she tried to fight back.

I saw the fear and hurt in my grandmother's eyes but could not comprehend it all to the fullest, I was too young. Here I am, me being a little child watching this I ask daddy because that's who he was to me, "are you angry at me too"? Then he cursed at me and threw a plate. Immediately I ran out the room and this was the first and only time I ever saw my grandmother leave my grandfather.

She was gone for two weeks and I was so afraid I learned not to speak because I saw speaking out to him could bring you great harm. Being there alone with him was strange I can't even remember where my oldest brother was because we both lived there but I remember this as though it was yesterday because it was the day that silenced me for years. I assumed if I didn't really talk or if I talked but said what people wanted to hear I would be safe. They would like me and it would be no trouble. This is when I became a people pleaser.

It was only until I took my strength back through prayer, fasting and talking to others that my no meant no and my yes meant yes.

So for years my I dealt with physical and verbal abuse, I accepted being treated like nothing because I felt like I was nothing. It seemed to me for a man to beat a woman must be ok after all when I looked all around me it seemed to be the norm.

So now the fear that pushed me in a corner and made me a people pleaser also left me with a mark of anger and rage. Although I dealt with low self-esteem I would fight, I became the one that used filthy language, screamed and yelled. Oh, wait I became the cheater, because I felt like I had been cheated on enough.

Fear and rejection became the number one plants in my life until I received Christ but that did not bring me my deliverance. I received deliverance when I understood I was now following the path of both my grandfather and grandmother along with others in my family and refused to except fear, rejection and anger as my companion.

I recognized that my adult issues stem from my childhood battles. Point here is I overcame fear and you can to. It doesn't matter what people are saying about you, they don't know your story and if they did some may not be able to handle it. I now walk in a great freedom because of Jesus Christ and you can to in each scripture you read meditate on what it is saying, pray and seek God's face and I believe that you will gain true joy.

Now we are on our way we have made it through the first Five days a representation of God's grace. He has given us the grace to stand and push through our storms. Remember each day you should try to journal. You will be amazed at how much stronger you will become.

Notes:

_____
_____
_____
_____
_____
_____
_____
_____
_____
_____
_____
_____
_____
_____
_____
_____
_____
_____
_____
_____
_____
_____
_____
_____
_____

Notes:

_____
_____
_____
_____
_____
_____
_____
_____
_____
_____
_____
_____
_____
_____
_____
_____
_____
_____
_____
_____
_____
_____
_____
_____
_____
_____
_____
_____
_____

Day 6 I can do all things

Philippians 4:12-13 12. I know both how to be abased and I know how to abound: everywhere and in all things, I am instructed both to be full and to be hungry, both to abound and to suffer need. 13. I can do all things through Christ which strengtheneth me.

Paul a man that gave up everything to obtain everything had been taught by the best. Paul a Pharisee one that was full of prestige and man's honor, gave it all up for Christ. After killing Gods people because he thought he was doing the desired work of God.

He found out that he didn't know the Lord like he thought because of self-righteousness the savior had come and he missed him, but he had an appointed time for what he would do.

God loved Paul he understood his flaws he knew what Paul would do and dealt with before Paul did. Why? Because he is God. Often, we live with guilt because of our past failures especially when we finally submit to God the enemy will try to keep you in the place of remembering when.

But Paul learned by submitting to God that he can have everything, or he cannot have everything, but he knew because he had Jesus through Christ he could do all things. Despite his past he had been forgiven. He counted everything he knew as nothing because Jesus became his personal instructor and loved him and showed him by saving him and accepting him.

The very one that was a killer, a murder of God people became the man God trusted to preach, teach and build his people. Paul learned how having and not having he gained understanding that the greatest gain was God.

Father we just magnify you today, wow you are incredible a God of no respect of person, you who love all and that desire all to come to the knowledge of the truth. I woke up and I understood I am forgiven and whatever my day holds I can do all things through Christ who strengthens me.

When I think about your goodness I become strong, when I get up my eyes open, my legs move I scream thank you Lord, you have won again. I can do anything with you in my life Jesus no one can stop me but me so today I put me to the side and surrender my spirit, soul and body unto you. I am only human but I am a human whose all powerful on the inside.

Oh my God we got this, I won't back up from you any longer but I run to you embracing your love you show towards me daily. Direct and instruct me Lord so that I may move according to your will. Thank you Father I have been made free and I will walk in my freedom and do the works of the Lord.

Notes:

Notes:

_____
_____
_____
_____
_____
_____
_____
_____
_____
_____
_____
_____
_____
_____
_____
_____
_____
_____
_____
_____
_____
_____
_____
_____
_____
_____
_____
_____

Day 7 A supplier

7. Philippians 4:19 But my God shall supply all your need according to his riches in glory by Christ Jesus.

Can I say today you ought to confess everything you can think of, that when you were in need God did it, just for you. It doesn't matter if it came from a man's hand God gave that person the mind to do it. The only time I have ever seen myself get frustrated with a need being supplied to me is when I put my hand in what God was trying to do for me.

All the time the needs that we meet are not God it is self-sustained which means we didn't wait on God. We tried to handle it ourselves and at the end of it there was a price to pay and we got angry with God trying to blame him for something we did by operating in man's wisdom rather than the wisdom of God. We couldn't wait for him to do it because we became too anxious. When we know that the word tells us to be anxious for nothing… (Philippians 4:6-7).

Listen our Father in heaven is rich there is know, I mean know good thing that he will withhold from us. God doesn't lie but man will if he had this man God write these words in the bible that was inspired by the Holy Ghost he means it. He shall supply all our needs according to his riches in glory by Christ Jesus.

Today ask yourself what his riches is, and what is in his glory that will be manifested by Christ Jesus. Which means whatever he has stored up in the heavens there will be an illumination of it made by Jesus. Remember all he has to say is let there be, and it shall be. Let's Pray

Lord you complete me and make me whole, you have always supplied my needs, when I cried you gave me joy, when I was weak you made me strong, you pull me out of depression and made me confident, today I need to just acknowledge you as my supplier of everything, my God you gave me peace in the midst of a mess, not only that but when I was hungry and thirsty you made a way out of no way. My bills were due I didn't see the way, but you made a way glory to your name God, truly when I look back over my life you have supplied my needs.

You Father clothe me and my family when we were in a tough spot, wait, you bless us with transportation whether with our own car or we got on a bus, funny but if we had to call for a cab it was you that enabled us to get it done. My, my, you supplied me with good health if I had a cold you blessed me to be healed. I don't want to ask for anything

Lord I just want to say thank you, thank you much. I have seen people robbed but you restore what was lost, whether is was spiritual or natural things. I have seen people shot, stabbed, in car accidents but you supplied them with life. I have been molested and talked about, called nothing but you supplied me with self-esteem and made me a new creature.

Lord Jesus today is a day of understanding how grateful I should be because not only have you supplied our needs, but you are yet supplying our needs. Only you can give life, save a soul, make someone feel brand new again. I am not worried about my daily bread because I know you will supply it. I won't worry about being talked about because you have given me the solution and that is to rejoice and be exceedingly glad.

Each day I recognize that there is nothing that has occurred in my life although it may have been hard sometimes you have always provided for me.

Thank you, Lord, In Jesus Christ name we continue to pray, Amen

Notes:

Notes:

Day 8 Made Free

Romans 6:20-22 20. For when ye were servants to sin, ye were free from righteousness. 21. What fruit had ye then in those things whereof ye are now ashamed? For the end of those things is death. 22. But now being made free from sin, and became servants to God, ye have your fruit unto holiness, and the end everlasting life.

There are things we did in life that man would say we deserve death but when we gave our lives over to Christ we died to self but, yet we became alive in Christ. Things that once had us bound we have now became free, free from sin and we now joyfully serve God. Rejoicing in the fact we have life eternally.

There is now nothing that will come before us that with God in our life we can't handle. Yes, it may seem difficult but when we had not Christ in our life it was truly nothing to look forward to accepting hell itself but now we live with our deliverer on the inside of us.

Take a moment and consider that fact without Christ all the heaviness and heartache we carried, we carried, but when we released ourselves to Christ no longer did we have to feel condemned or ashamed for whom the son of man set free is truly again free indeed.

I have been made free from sin and I walk as a servant of God. I submit and surrender to his will. My fruit is righteous and truly I rejoice because I has everlasting life. Because my God is he that makes me who I am, kingdom made,

Kingdom born, despite the past issues I may have had today I am kingdom called.
Washed in the blood of the Lamb
Thank you, Jesus for shedding your blood on my behalf.
Amen

Notes:

Notes:

Day 9 Rest in Christ

Proverbs 3:24-26 When thou liest down, thou shalt not be afraid, yea, thou shalt lie down, and thy sleep shall be sweet. 25. Be not afraid of sudden fear, neither of desolation of the wicked, when it cometh. 26. For the Lord shall be thy confidence and shall keep thy foot from being taken.

Father in the name of Jesus as I lay down to rest I will not fear neither shall I be troubled. My spirit, soul and body belong to you, tonight I bind the works and operations of witches, warlocks, sorcerer's, Satanist, hoodoo and voodoo workers.

Confound the mind of the enemy oh Lord disrupt the meetings of the root workers, seal our home dear Lord and block the way of every astral projector, channeler and water craft worker, we cut them down even now in Jesus name. We release Holy Ghost fire that it may burn up every ungodly altar in the name of Jesus. I confess my sleep will be sweet tonight every eye of the enemy will be blinded and is blinded even now scanners and watchers you are blocked with Holy Ghost fire in Jesus name. I am confident that I am covered with the blood of Jesus for I am a child of God.

We apply the blood of Jesus over ourselves through the power of the Holy Ghost. We speak into the atmosphere and release the anointing of God as we seek him to release the angels of protection about our lives. I shall not be overtaken by the enemy for the Lord is my strength in Jesus name, Amen

Notes:

Notes:

Day 10   Fear is not an option

Luke 12:4-5 And I say unto you my friends, be not afraid of them that kill the body, and after that have no more that they can do. 5. But I forewarn you whom ye shall fear: Fear Him, which after he hath killed hath power to cast into hell; yea, I say unto you Fear him.

Now is not the time to fear people. Sure, they will try to push fear in you with threats, yelling, bullying and other tactics that you may walk with a respect for them that come from terror. They carry only the power that you allow them to have and hold over your life.

Let your concern be with Christ to honor him, respect him because he is God and he is the only one that has a heaven or hell to place you in. He breathes life into you each day. It is Christ that gives us witty ideas and inventions, it is he that will be with us even until the end of the world. Today break free from fearing what man will say or do to you.

Lord here I am seeking you, you are a mighty God an awesome Father and friend to me. Forgive me Lord for allowing myself to be intimidated by others. Jesus, I have always found you to be my strength I will not fear man, but I will walk boldly through you.

All praises and glory belong to you and I lift my hands to you in total submission acknowledging that you are my strength. I will not fear the terror by night nor arrows that fly by day. In you there is my secret place, my hiding spot when I come to you cover me with your wings. This day oh God I shall gird myself with your strength and continue to cast down and renounce any fear that man has tried to place in me. I declare my peace in you, so I will keep my mind on you and meditate upon your word both day and night. Thank you, Father, for just being God, in Jesus name, Amen

Notes:

Notes:

_____
_____
_____
_____
_____
_____
_____
_____
_____
_____
_____
_____
_____
_____
_____
_____
_____
_____
_____
_____
_____
_____
_____
_____
_____
_____

Day 11 Validated by Christ

Isaiah 51:7 Hearken unto me, ye that know righteousness, the people in whose heart is my law. Fear ye not the reproach of men, neither be ye afraid of their reviling's. 8. For the moth shall eat them up like a garment, and the worm shall eat them like wool: but my righteousness shall be forever, and my salvation from generation to generation.

Many times, we are looking to be accepted by others waiting to be validated through their words. Waiting for them to approve our belief our faith in God. Here the Prophet Isaiah says, listen to me you that know righteousness. You understand living right and you have hidden the laws of God in your heart.

Do not I repeat do not be afraid of those that put forth a disapproval, or disgrace concerning you neither be afraid of their abusive language. They won't last, God will deal with them and they will be eaten alive. But the righteousness of God will be forever and his salvation, deliverance well it will go from one generation to the next.

Lord I now praise you because daily I am conquering the fears that has been placed in me. I will not wait for man to approve of my faith but rather I will hearken unto you and follow your righteousness. It is you that will comfort your people and judge us according to your word. You are Maker that has stretched forth heaven and laid the foundations of the earth.

My spirit has been awakened through you and I am getting stronger day by day. I now take authority over the spirit of fear, fear of not being accepted by others and worrying about their disapproval of my faith, lifestyle, the way I dress, speak, walk or talk whatever the disapproval has been. I bind up abusive words, contemptuous words right now in Jesus name. Amen

Notes:

Notes:

Day 12 Fret Not

Psalm 37:1-3; 39-40 1. Fret not thyself because of evildoers, neither be thou envious against the workers of iniquity. 2. For they shall soon be cut down like the grass and wither as the green herb, 3. Trust in the Lord, and do good; so, shall thy dwell on the land, and verily thou shalt be fed.

39.But the salvation of the righteous is of the Lord: he is their strength in the time of trouble. 40. And the Lord shall help them and deliver them: he shall deliver them from the wicked, and save them, because they trust in him.

We must always be ready to walk in the righteousness of God it is the only way, even though the wicked may appear to prosper and hold great power they will pass away and not be found.

Those that are complete in God their end shall be peace. To many times we focus on what people have, what people say, and we lose total sight of the Lord. What has the word said of us, and what did his word say about those who live for Him.

As you begin to pray our focus will be on Psalm 37 for we will Fret not.

Lord we just bless you, we praise you and magnify you, you God are the King of Glory and to be in your presence is a delight to my soul. Oh, how I worship and adore you, I love you Lord simply because you are God. Thank you in advance for moving consistently and continuously in my life.

On this day we declare that we will not fret because of those that walk-in wickedness and appear to prosper for we know that they will soon be cut down. We are the walking church the temple of God. Our eyes are on you and we do trust in you.

Father we are committed to turning from any wickedness in our lives striving to do good. This day we declare that we will live in the land of plenty and be fed by you. We declare we will delight our hearts in you and seek to your face faithfully not for things but for you and we thank you now for giving us the desires of heart.

Right now, I commit my way unto you for truly I cannot walk this life out alone I trust you with not only my life but with my family, friends and foes. If you have spoken a word I know surely it will come to pass.

I renounce this anger for I am of you and yes I understand I can be angry and not go overboard but anger has tried to run rapid in my life so I release it out of my life, vengeance is not to preform. I will not be jealous of others and envious of them with the naked eye because it looks as if they are in the best place in life. Today anger must go, jealousy go, envy go, frustration go in Jesus name.

I acknowledge that these things have tried to take hold of my life, but my heart is for God and I will not allow these things to separate me from my Father. I bind the spirit of peace, love and joy to my heart and command the fruit of spirit to flow. I declare I am the righteousness of God. I will whole heartily trust the Lord, thou the wicked come to together speaking evil, and even when they devise wicked actions towards us, the Lord is laughing for he knows the wicked's time is short. But the Lord knows the way of the righteous will be forever.

I am free to live and receive all that the Lord has for me in Jesus name

Notes:

_____
_____
_____
_____
_____
_____
_____
_____
_____
_____
_____
_____
_____
_____
_____
_____
_____
_____
_____
_____
_____
_____
_____
_____
_____
_____

Notes:

Day 13 My face is set

Isaiah 50:4-7 The Lord God has given me the tongue of the learned, that I should know how to speak a word in season to him that is weary: he wakens morning by morning, he wakens my ear to hear as the learned. 5. The Lord hath open mine ear; and I was not rebellious, neither turned away back. 6. I gave my back to the smiters, and my cheeks to them that plucked off the hair: I hid not my face from shame and spitting. 7. For the Lord God will help me; therefore, shall I not be confounded: therefore, have I set my face like a flint, and I know I shall not be ashamed.

Isaiah speaks a prophetic word here speaking on Christ's behalf our King and Messiah in verses four through eleven. The Messiah was coming, and this is what Isaiah spoke of him. In the earlier verses one through three God spoke that he wanted to fight on Israel's behalf, but they sold out to sin they hindered what could be done.

We must not rebel against the word of God but rather trust and obey his word. It has never been God's desire not to fight for us, love and care for us but when we step out on our own we tie his hands. God is so loving when Isaiah begin to speak. He has given me the tongue of the learned that I should know how to speak a word in season to him that is weary…

Listen the Lord wants to give us a timely word to speak in the lives of others and not just for ourselves. Look around you, we have family members, people that are sleeping in cars on the streets, gang bangers, church folk, children, drug dealers, and those that are bond by drugs or different illnesses.

These people need a word that will give them strength to make it and God has given us that word to speak into someone else's life. The word describes the Messiah, it says he was not rebellious but gave willingly off his back to the smiters that was done for you and me.

They snatched the hairs from his cheeks he took that for us, Jesus knew the Father as his help as we today should know whatever the issues are when we submit to God he is our help. We don't have to be confused Jesus was not confused his eyes was set like a flint which simply means he had a made-up mine that the devil in hell would lose the fight.

His assignment was greater then rejection and rebellion of the people. He was not ashamed of what he had to deal with each day. His ear was open to hear the Father as our ears should be open to receive what God has to say to us that we may be directed in the path of God.

Our focus must be on God he will always give us what to say and do if we only can trust him. If there has been rebellion in our lives, we must renounce it and submit unto the righteousness of God. Our Savior confidently took on every burden we would have to bear. If we follow him, we are strong but it is when we try to fly solo that we become powerless.

Precious Jesus we praise your name and we speak over the lives of others and ourselves that we will not walk in rebellion, but we will submit unto your word. We have always known you to be our help. We declare today that you shall continue to be our help and that we will continue submit unto to your word.

Our ears are open each morning waiting to receive instruction and guidance from you that we may be able to bless those that are weary. Forever oh God our hearts will be toward you for you have given us the tongue of the learned and we are thankful.

Our ears have been open to your truth we reject the lying words of the enemy and we accept the truth of God. You will fight on our behalf those that are weak and weary, families that have been torn apart, those that are lame not just physically but have become cripple in the spirit. Oh my God we will not run in our own strength, but we wait patiently for you. In Jesus name

Notes:

Notes:

Notes:

Day 14 God my everything

Psalms 138:7-8 Though I walk in the midst of trouble, thou wilt revive me: thou shalt stretch forth thine hand against the wrath of mine enemies, and thy right hand shall save me. 8. The Lord will perfect that which concerneth me: thy mercy, O Lord, endures forever: forsake not the works of thine own hands.

It is so amazing that no matter what we read in the word of God we find that He is a life sustainer, a God of strength, truth, love and hope. God's word helps us to understand he complete things that are concerning us.

To my great and awesome God, we praise your name continually. Each day we awaken we will remember the times of our trouble, you, like a bolt of electricity quicken me and made my life meaningful. We praise you because you prospered us, kept us from fainting, you have given us life. Lord areas we are under developed and or immature you have loved us enough to mature us in you. You love and made those things in our life that where unfulfilled be fulfilled.

You are our blessed assurance. Despite the broken relationships are painstaking disappointments in our life. I yet praise you for I know that trouble may come but it will also go, thank you for hastening to perform your word and watching over us. I declare I will praise you always. I declare God is our sustainer.I declare our day to be glorious and prosper.I declare that in which was started in my life shall be fulfilled. In Jesus name, Amen

Notes:

_____

_____

_____

_____

_____

_____

_____

_____

_____

_____

_____

_____

_____

_____

_____

_____

_____

_____

_____

_____

_____

_____

Notes:

Day 15 Mercy

Psalms 57:1 Be merciful unto me, O God, be merciful unto me: for my soul trusteth in thee: yea, in the shadow of thy wings will I make my refuge, until these calamities be over past. 2. I will cry unto God most high; unto God that performeth all things for me.

Have you ever been in a position when the only thing you could do is seek God for his mercy? It appears if anything could happen in your life it did happen. There was no one around to comfort you but you, so you thought.

I have experienced over the years seeing people in such a struggle that they felt like everyone was against them and they had no one. The truth is they had God they simply had to see that he was there all the time waiting for them to call so that he may answer them. There is no battle to great for God so seek him for a hiding place.

The word declares when there none other to encourage David he encouraged himself and called for the ephod in sought the Lord. Whatever you need it is in Jesus Christ, you were born to overcome and win through Christ. Release whatever it is and walk in victory today.

I recognize that you are a God full of mercy dear Lord, so I will trust in you, my soul trust in you. Father continue to cover me, for you Lord are hiding place, shelter in the time of storms.

I declare you to be my protector keeping me from dangers seen and unseen. I declare all things are now being performed for me through you. I apply the most Holy blood of Jesus over my children let now oh God your mercy find them and your arm of protection cover them. I will continue to raise them up in the way of righteousness be with them and Lord those that are grown and have been taught your ways Father stir them up on the inside they may walk upright before you.

We speak now that every generational curse be broken, every self-induced curse be broken. Let your mercy flow right now even as I call upon your name Jesus let every ungodly altar be burned with Holy Ghost fire, Altars that we have built in our hearts we release the oil of God over our children and grandchildren, our children, children's, children's.

We declare the altars are torn down, generational curses are broken, and the mercy of God is hiding us even now. In Jesus name

Note:

Notes:

Day 16 The good work

Philippians 3:1-11

3. I thank my God in all my remembrance of you, 4. always in every prayer of mine for you all making my prayer with joy, 5. because of your partnership in the gospel from the first day until now. 6. And I am sure of this, that he who began a good work in you will bring it to completion at the day of Jesus Christ. 7. It is right for me to feel this way about you all, because I hold you in my heart, for you are all partakers with me of grace, both in my imprisonment and in the defense and confirmation of the gospel. 8. For God is my witness, how I yearn for you all with the affection of Christ Jesus. 9. And it is my prayer that your love may abound more and more, with knowledge and all discernment, 10. so that you may approve what is excellent, and so be pure and blameless for the day of Christ, 11. filled with the fruit of righteousness that comes through Jesus Christ, to the glory and praise of God.

Paul prayed this prayer concerning the Philippians knowing that he did not walk in grace alone but the grace of God he shared and partook in it together and his heart was toward them and their growth in God.

He encourages them by saying this, he had confidence that he who started the work would complete the work. Can you say today God will complete the work in not only your life, but somebody name before God and declare the work shall be complete in their lives.

We declare our love will grow daily and He that has begun a good work shall complete it not only in me but in_____

We declare that we will strive to walk with greater discernment as I grow in love.

Take a moment and think about all the places in your life God is developing and maturing you. As well as people your heart is towards. Believe God will finish the work in your life declare that you forgive and have been forgiven daily and every good thing and every righteous belong to you. Declare over your today you are victorious you are a winner in Jesus name.

Notes:

_____
_____
_____
_____
_____
_____
_____
_____
_____
_____
_____
_____
_____
_____
_____
_____
_____
_____
_____
_____
_____
_____
_____
_____
_____

Notes:

Day 17 Speak Wise

Proverbs 10:27-32 The fear of the Lord prolongeth days: but the years of the wicked shall be shortened. 28. The hope of the righteous shall be gladness: but the expectation of the wicked shall perish. 29. The way of the Lord is strength to the upright: but destruction shall be to, the workers of iniquity. 30. The righteous shall never be removed: but the wicked shall not inhabit the earth. 31. The mouth of the just bring forth wisdom: but forward tongue shall be cut out. 32. The lips of the righteous know what is acceptable: but the mouth of the wicked speaketh forwardness.

Today we confess that our days will be prolonged, because we fear you, we will not walk in wickedness.

We confess our hope is in the gladness of knowing who you are in our lives, we will not ponder on self-indulgent desires.

We confess that we have chosen your way in life and have become stronger through you, for our ways are not your ways, so we can graciously acknowledge today that our ways can weaken us but the way of the Lord will always make us strong. For we will lean not upon what we think or know but we will lean on you our Lord our God and our Savior.

We confess we are like trees planted by the rivers of water we shall not be moved for we declare to be the trees of righteousness

We confess our tongues to be wise we will speak the wisdom of God and we will not walk with corrupt communication destroying ourselves and others.

We confess that we know what is acceptable to speak and we will set a watch before our mouths. Guarding our lips that we speak that which is good and acceptable in the sight of God.

This is the day that the Lord has made so we will rejoice and be glad in it. Glory to God!!!

Notes:

Notes:

Day 18 My Shepherd

Psalms 23 The Lord is my Shepherd I shall not want. 2.He make to lie down beside the still waters. 3. He restoreth my soul: he leadeth me in the paths of righteousness for his name's sake. 4. Yea, though I walk through the valley of the shadows of death, I will fear no evil: for thou art with me; thy rod and thy staff they comfort me. 5. Thou preparest a table before me in the presence of mine enemies: thou anoint my head with oil; my cup run over. 6. Surely goodness and mercy shall follow me all the days of my life: and Ii will dwell in the house of the Lord forever.

Although many of us grew up hearing this particular division of Psalm we spoke but, yet it never really penetrated our hearts. David describes God as being a Shepherd one that will supply all needs, he provides shelter, clothing, water and food, he gives peace, and will refresh us as needed, the moments that are dark and difficult we do not have to fear any evil, for the Lord has declared he will never leave us nor forsake us, he is with us.

He will bless us right in the very mist of our prosecutors, false accusers, and enemies whose entire job is to attempt to destroy us. He will use his rod to correct us and staff to fight off the hand of our enemies. He will anoint our head with oil; meaning the Lord will empower us himself, we will overflow with power. The goodness and mercy of God will follow us and I AM FULLY CONFIDENT, I am persuaded in this, the Lord being our Shepherd we will easily follow Him all the days of our lives and reside in his house forever.

We declare God as our Shepherd and there is nothing in this life we shall want.

My soul has been restored, because my God he has lead us unto the path of righteousness, Amen

Notes:

Notes:

_____
_____
_____
_____
_____
_____
_____
_____
_____
_____
_____
_____
_____
_____
_____
_____
_____
_____
_____
_____
_____
_____
_____
_____
_____
_____
_____

Day 19 My Helper

Psalms 54:4; 6-7

4. Behold, God is mine helper: The Lord is with them that uphold my soul.

6. I will freely sacrifice unto thee: I will praise thy name, O Lord; for it is good. 7. For he hath delivered me out of all trouble and mine eye hath seen his desire upon mine enemies.

There is a call for God to overcome our enemies David has always understood that God was his help and his feelings where always freely expressed to the Lord if he needed help he asked for it, if he was troubled he expressed that, if he was excited and needed to repent David also did that but at the end of his request he always gave God praise he honored him and recognized that his deliverance was now.

When we speak to God and release our concerns in the atmosphere the Lord begin to go to work on behalf of his children. We not always see an immediate change but as we speak to God and release things He will release things from heaven.

Our enemy is not people although the devil, Satan uses people as his instrument to get his job done. When we talk to the Lord we are not, nor should we ever pray against or about people, but about the situation. Then you can joyfully watch God bring you out of your troubles.

We declare that God is our help. We declare that God is covering those that are covering us.

We declare that we will freely without hesitation praise the name of God.

We declare it is good to sacrifice and praise God.
We declare that we will rest in the fact that God has
unequivocally delivered us out trouble.
We declare that every demonic spirit will eyes see be cast out
of those the enemy has used.
We declare our joy and peace in God will remain in our
hearts in Jesus name, Amen
Father we bless you and praise you forever more.

Notes:

_____
_____
_____
_____
_____
_____
_____
_____
_____
_____
_____
_____
_____
_____
_____
_____
_____
_____
_____
_____
_____
_____
_____
_____
_____

Notes:

Day 20 A call to destiny

Deuteronomy 31:7-8 And Moses called unto Joshua and said unto him in the sight of all Israel, Be strong and of a good courage: for thou must go with this people unto the land which the Lord hath sworn unto their Fathers to give them; and thou shalt cause them to inherit it. 8. And the Lord, he it is that doth go before thee; he will be with thee, he will not fail thee, neither forsake thee: fear not, neither be dismayed.

Let's look at these two passages we all have dealt with many types of fear, but this is a fear of walking into purpose, destiny a place of calling.

Moses had been faithful to the call of God and Joshua had been faithful the servant of God. He saw the good, bad and ugly first hand. He had faith when ten spies saw giants in the promise land. Joshua said we can do this, isn't something we feel powerful about when someone else is responsible for being in the leadership position but when God wants to elevate you the fear of rejection and failure set in.

God want us to face the giants and he want us to not be afraid and worried. We have been trained for this just like Joshua was. He may not have even understood all that was sown in his life until he was called to use a different level of fight and leadership qualities.

Today let's cast down fear of failure and being failed. The power of goodness and mercy follows us but it is God himself that goes before us.

Let's pray

Precious Jesus we will not fear destiny and purpose in our life we realize all these things that we have been challenged with has been to prepare us to be the leaders you wanted us to be, whether on the job, in the church or in school.

We now kill the giants that have tried to consume our lives. That giant that said I will follow but never will I lead. That giant that said I can kill the enemy only with my Moses around. I confess that I am full of Holy Ghost power and even as Moses spoke into Joshua's life to be strong and of good courage so shall I be in Jesus name.

I declare I am strong and not weak.

I declare I am bold and not afraid.

I declare I will not worry but be confident in God.

I declare I will run to my destiny and not from it.

I cast down every fear the enemy would want to paralyze me with. I burn it with Holy Ghost fire. In Jesus name.

Notes:

_____
_____
_____
_____
_____
_____
_____
_____
_____
_____
_____
_____
_____
_____
_____
_____
_____
_____
_____
_____
_____
_____
_____
_____
_____
_____

Notes:

Day 21   Salvation of the Righteous

Psalms 37:39-40 But the salvation of the righteous is of the Lord: he is their strength in the time of trouble. 40. And the Lord shall help them, from the wicked, and save them, because they trust in him.

In the 37 division of Psalms there is so much to look at, but the meat of it simply describes what happens to the righteous and the unrighteous. In here the word declares in verse 23 the steps of a good man are ordered by the Lord: and he (speaking of God) delighted in his ways. Verse 24 It says, though he falls, he shall not be utterly cast down: for the Lord upholdeth him with his hand.

David here again is the speaker in this division of Psalms he had clear understanding we do not see what the Lord sees. David was undeserving of righteousness to a natural mans eye but to God he was a man after his own heart. Why, was this so? David was an adulterer, murderer, deceiver and he was one that manipulated his situation but, yet God loved him, forgave him and caused him to reign over his people.

We are moving into a place of clarity now as we look at David's life before we go into prayer. We will briefly look at a few things concerning him, he was a young shepherd boy that gain his experiences by guarding natural sheep.

He killed a bear and a lion. He loved God, in his heart was a greater commitment to the Lord then all his brothers. They were afraid of Goliath but not David he had such a faith in God until it hurt him for someone to speak against God. So, he fought against the giant that everyone else ran from, slew him in the name of our God.

Point is David heart was for God and God saw what no one else saw. He was warrior for the Lord and he sought the Lord diligently with his whole heart. David understood he had flaws and he also understood that God could deliver, forgive and set free. He knew God was full of mercy, so he advised us to depart from evil and do good.

The Lord will never forsake his people believe it or not righteous people make major mistakes and sometimes it is simply bad choices and decisions. Question, have you ever been there where you made a horrible choice, but God loved you so much he sent someone to you to bring you back to the face of God? Maybe he gave you a dream or you read his word, or it could have been a still small voice; but he let you know to do good and turn from evil for he loves you and he will bring you out of your mess and built you up continually for his purpose.

David understood that God could not only deliver him for his wickedness but from the wickedness of others. Let us begin to focus on breaking the chains off of our lives less we stay in darkness assuming that we are walking in the light of God. Remember even good people make poor choices but it does not mean they are not loved by God, accepted by God or God is not with them. If he can love you and forgive you surely, he can love everyone else.

Prayer for today: Lord we glorify you right now declaring that evil has no part in us, knowing the salvation of the righteous of the Lord. We declare that we are of the righteous.

God, we recognize that you are our strength we continually confess it and release it in the atmosphere seeing and knowing we are covered in your blood and we are forgiven even as David was forgiven.

There is nothing in our past that we will allow to hinder our future we are free in Christ Jesus. We declare our deliverance is through you and we have been delivered from the wicked and from the wickedness that was within us.

You are righteous judge, never have you forsaken the saints of God. Today I proclaim I am a saint of God, you shall preserve me forever in Jesus name, Amen

Notes:

Notes:

Day 22 A praise of Peace

Isaiah 26:3-4 Thou wilt keep him in perfect peace, whose mind is stayed on thee: because he trusteth in thee. 4. Trust ye in the Lord forever: for int the Lord Jehovah is everlasting strength.

Isaiah is speaking a word that of continual praise that a song shall be sung, a joyful sound shall be made because of the spiritual walls that will be coming down. There are walls that I declare are coming down now in your life rejoice and believe that you are a child of God and despite the continual warfare, we declare that the battle is coming to an end and we are walking in the peace of God.

Oh Lord, my Father which art in heaven we honor you today and thank you for your peace a peace that surpasses all understanding. I long to have your peace always not as the world will offer it but that everlasting peace that bubbles on the inside of me. I declare peace today now Lord in my home, on my job. I declare peace in my family, I speak it and declare it to be so for this is the power that you have given me to speak life into dry places.

I declare rivers of peace flowing again in my life. I will keep my mind stayed on you and in doing so I know you will keep me in perfect peace. I declare peace that I have obtained through our Lord Jesus Christ.

So Lord I will follow peace with all men and knowing without holiness no man shall see the Lord. Lord at the appointed time I shall see you for with long life you shall satisfy me. I will live until I am satisfied in you Lord and walk diligently in your peace.

Notes:

Notes:

_____

_____

_____

_____

_____

_____

_____

_____

_____

_____

_____

_____

_____

_____

_____

_____

_____

_____

_____

_____

_____

Day 23 Praises of the Redeemed

Isaiah 25:1; 4

1. O Lord, thou art my God; I will exalt thee, I will praise thy name; for thou hast done wonderful things; thou counsel of old are faithfulness and truth.

4. For thou hast been a strength to the poor, a strength to the needy in his distress, a refuge from the storm, a shadow from the heat, when a blast of the terrible ones is as a storm against the wall.

The Lord is coming back, and he is coming for his children. He knows about your troubles and the things you have suffered and those things he will deal with because of you suffering. Praise the Lord for who he is today and what he will always be a never changing and forever loving God.

Father we exalt you and praise your name for you have done wonderful things, you have been faithful and true in the past and even now; we can't help but praise such an honorable and righteous God. Who does what you have done? You made man from the ground you made woman from the rib of the man.

Even in the falling of man you had a plan all along to redeem your children back unto the Father. Lord we adore you, you have been and still are strength for the poor and needy. We declare you to be our refuge when we don't know where to run, we will always run to the rock of our salvation.

We confess in our distress you have been there, in the midst of the storm you hide us beneath your wings. I declare you to be my peaceful hiding place. I am not troubled there nor am I afraid. I will rejoice in the Lord today and glorify him for he has not forgotten us the shall bring down the pride of the unrighteous and tear down the wall of the enemy. To God be the glory in Jesus name.

Notes:

Notes:

Day 24 He will keep me

Isaiah 43:1-2 But now thus saith the Lord that created thee, O Jacob, and he that formed thee, O Israel, Fear not: for I have redeemed thee, I have called thee by thy name; thy art mine, 2. When thou pass through the waters, I will be with thee; and through the rivers, they shall not overflow thee: when thou walkest through the fire, thou shalt not be burned; neither shall the flame kindle upon thee.

Amazingly in the midst of our disobedience God, although he disciplines us he still gives us reassurance that he is with us. The Lord had to reassure Israel that despite of how they let him down he wasn't going to let them down. There are things we may deal with that we may want to blame it all on a person, a job, a store clerk.

Yes, we can point at everyone but ourselves saying if they would not have done this then this would not have happened. Well listening in my spirit if you would have obeyed God then he would not have had to allow the enemy to have at you. He did not let hurts and pains destroy you but rather help you to understand that there is nobody like our God and it is important to obey him.

Rejecting God can put us in a place of feeling rejected by him and other's when truly it's not that. The fact is that you have opened a door through your hatred, bitterness, resentment, unforgiveness, lust, lies, deceit, lack of trust and other things so the devil have a legal right to your life. God loved Israel, so he let them know don't fear because rest assure you may have gone through but those that put you through, even if I release them on you will pay. Now don't rejoice over that but rejoice in the fact despite your messy self he still got your back and has given you a chance to serve Him.

Father thank you for being with us in the flaws in our life even in the mist of rejecting you, you kept us. The fire did not burn us we came out worn but not destroyed. I declare you have called me by name and never will a flood over take me, never will the fire burn me. I am shielded by your love and covered in the blood of Jesus.

Your blood has washed me cleansed me. I declare boldness in my life I shall not fear for you Lord are on my side. I declare my family that is scattered abroad will be brought together by you. I speak salvation over my family this day in Jesus name. Disobedience caused us to go different places like the children of Israel were scattered so were we, but we speak togetherness in Jesus holy name.

We declare to know that God is the great I am and besides him there is no other. We renounce disobedience now and cast down every idol in Jesus name

Thank you, Father for covering us, saving us often from our own selves. My life is in your hands and I willfully submit unto you.

Notes:

Notes:

_____
_____
_____
_____
_____
_____
_____
_____
_____
_____
_____
_____
_____
_____
_____
_____
_____
_____
_____
_____
_____
_____
_____
_____
_____

Day 25 Overcoming the world

1 John 5:4 For whatsoever is born of God overcome the world: and this is the victory that overcome the world, even our faith. 5. Who is he that overcome the world, but he that believe that Jesus is the Son of God.

Father, in the name of Jesus we thank you for giving us strength this day to overcome obstacles that may have been placed in our way. We have already overcome them for whatsoever is born of God overcome this world: I have faith and believe that you Jesus are the Son of God. So now I have been overcome by the blood of the lamb and the words of my testimony. I speak victory into my day through my Lord and Savior.

I honor you today for Lord you have never left me nor forsaken me, you are the lover of my soul. It is in you I live, move and have my being. Lord I adore you Father God. Help me that I may always keep the fight, the good fight of faith.

Empower others today that maybe struggling within themselves feeling as though no one cares. Jesus let your love be made known to them by others that are surrounding them throughout this day. Help us Lord on this day that we walk with your heart of love and with a heart of gratitude. Be for us, for if you be for us who can be against us in Jesus name we pray, Amen

1 John 5:4-5; Revelations 12:11; Timothy 6:12

Notes:

_____
_____
_____
_____
_____
_____
_____
_____
_____
_____
_____
_____
_____
_____
_____
_____
_____
_____
_____
_____
_____
_____
_____
_____
_____
_____

Notes:

_____
_____
_____
_____
_____
_____
_____
_____
_____
_____
_____
_____
_____
_____
_____
_____
_____
_____
_____
_____
_____
_____
_____
_____

Day 26 My God gives me beauty

Isaiah 61:3 … To give them beauty for ashes, the oil of joy for mourning, the garment of praise for the spirit of heaviness; that they may be called the trees of righteousness, the planting of the Lord, that he may glorified.

I declare I am beautiful and all ashes have been removed.
I declare I am full of the oil of Joy.
I declare I wear a garment of praise.
I declare I have been planted as a tree of righteousness.

Lord in your name Father we say thank you. Thank you for keeping us throughout the night, for keeping us from dangers seen and unseen. We bless your holy name for you are great and greatly to be praised. What or who can be compared to you, your love that you have shone towards us is so incredible.

We shout glory to your holy name. Wonderful, Counselor, Mighty God, Everlasting Father is what you are, healer for the sick, peace for the broken, joy for those in sorry. Thank you for giving us beauty for ashes, the oil of joy for mourning, the spirit of praise for the spirit of heaviness.

Who else would do that for us that we might be called the trees of righteousness? Oh Father with a grateful heart we say thank you and there is no doubt in our heart that you will be for us today.

Thank you for hearing us always in Jesus name

Isaiah 61:3; 1 Thessalonians 5:18, Isaiah 9:6

Notes:

_____
_____
_____
_____
_____
_____
_____
_____
_____
_____
_____
_____
_____
_____
_____
_____
_____
_____
_____
_____
_____
_____

Notes:

Day 27 Receive Power

Acts 1:8 But ye shall receive power, after that the Holy Ghost is come upon: and ye shall be witnesses unto me both in Jerusalem, and in all Judea, and in Samaria, and unto the uttermost part of the earth.

Prayer:

Father we thank you once again for waking us up on this wonderful day. We continue to glorify you for you are spectacular, incredible and truly indescribable. We honor you oh Father, how great is our God, you are a great God and all the earth is now awaiting your great return Lord Jesus.

This is yet another day Lord that you are calling your children higher. So, Lord we ask in the name of Jesus that you empower us from on high. We speak and release the power of Christ within us through the authority that was placed within us when we received the Holy Ghost.

Your word Lord declared that after the Holy Ghost has come upon us we would receive power. Today we stir up the power in us. We speak even a stronger Godly fear in our lives for it brings forth wisdom and knowledge, honoring you Lord allows us to hear you even more for we respect that which you speak into our ears.

We will not be dull of hearing, but we will acknowledge you that you may direct us in each path we take. Be for us Lord for if you be for us who can be against us. Let not the enemy triumph over us, enlighten us that we may see that we be not tricked by the hands of the enemy. We love and honor you

Lord we will walk in the beauty of holiness today and forever.

Acts 1:8 Proverbs 3: 5-6   Psalms 25:2-5 Proverbs 1:7 Proverbs 4:7

Notes:

Notes:

Day 28 Stand

1 Corinthians 16:13 Watch ye, stand fast in the faith, quit you like men, be strong. 14.Let all your things be done with charity.

God wants us to be alert and aware of things, to be strong in our faith not shaken or moved, respectful to man's relationship with the Father honor who he is. We are to behave like his children and be strong not allowing fear and intimidation to overtake us. In everything we do it must be with Godly love. We cannot choose who to love but we must love all mankind.

Our spirit is open, and we are watching daily being alert and aware of all things.
We act like the children of God and are strong.
In all that we do we do it is in love even as Christ has loved us.
Father even now we yet praise you for we are stronger than we have ever been. We have matured in a place of knowing how to walk as the children of God and not move as a novice. Though I confess life had shaken me and I was discouraged I praise you now. For I can love others now, stand strong in faith and claim my victory like never. I respect your word for it is you therefore Jesus I respect and honor you. I will move in this day strong and confident alert and aware knowing that you Lord has taken care of everything. Even as I surrender my will unto you I know that you will guide me, protect me and give me what I need to say and help me to hold my tongue when it can damage others.

Praising you always and loving every minute of it, In Jesus name Amen

Notes:

Notes:

Day 29 The light is shining

2 Corinthians 4:6-11 6. For God, who commanded the light to shine out of a darkness, hath shined in our hearts, to give light of the knowledge of the glory of God in the face of Jesus Christ 7. But we have this treasure in earthen vessels, that the excellency of the power may be of God and not of us. 8. We are troubled on every side, yet not distressed; we are perplexed, but not in despair, 9. Persecuted, but not forsaken, cast down, but not destroyed; 10. Always bearing about in the body the dying of the Lord Jesus, that the life also of Jesus might he made manifest in our body.

Beloved this passage of scripture are so powerful. First, the word says, God commanded light this wasn't a suggestion but a command no option that light would shine out of darkness, it didn't say shine on darkness but in a dark place. Jesus who is the light shines through this darkness, what was the darkness it was the darkness of our soul and Jesus himself removed sin and became a shining light in us.

Opening our minds to understand the illuminating power of God in the face of Jesus Christ. His light gave us an assurance that we walked with power. You see to, stand in power you must have power, the power of the Holy Ghost. When the light shines out of a dark place darkness flees.

Depression runs, and the joy of the Lord becomes your strength. Unforgiveness begin to melt away because love begins to cover, and bitterness wanted to destroy. Weariness fades because the understand that we will reap if we faint not.

We declare we carry the treasure the word of God within us, that the excellency of the power may be of God and not of us.

We declare that we are not distressed, and trouble will not overwhelm us.

We declare we are full of hope and we denounce hopelessness.

We declare we have been supported and looked after by God for his word is true. He would never leave us nor forsake us, we renounce the spirit of abandonment and feeling forsaken.

We declare that we shall stand in adversity and not me ruin by man's actions are opinion.

We declare we carry daily the evidence of our resurrected Savior in our life by allowing his wonderful light to shine through us.

Notes:

Notes:

_____

_____

_____

_____

_____

_____

_____

_____

_____

_____

_____

_____

_____

_____

_____

_____

_____

_____

_____

_____

_____

_____

_____

_____

Day 30 Love in Truth

1 John 3:15-18 Whosoever hateth his brother is a murderer: and ye know that no murderer hath eternal life abiding in him. 16. Hereby perceive we the love of God, because he laid down his life for us: and we ought to lay down our lives for the brethren.

This is a strong message of the importance of true love and the danger of hatred. When God is speaking here concerning a murder he is really talking of a person that has not repented nor turned from his wickedness but has chosen to continue to kill.

We can murder with our mouth choosing to destroy lives daily which says there is no eternal life for those that choose to live like that. It is the same way with hate God compares a person full of hate to murderer.

These are some of the things someone who hates and someone who is a murderer have in common you can't trust others, you do not rest well, you will be negative, short fused, lying, always trying to find faults with others and your mouth becomes the main killer.

Lord we renounce hate and grab hold of your love.

We declare we will not destroy others with our words but rather promote life by showing love.

We declare that we will not ignore the needs of our brothers when it is in our power to help.

We declare we love in deed and in truth.

Father as we declare your love in our lives we say thank you so much for teaching us our ways are not yours. Lord your love is so powerful that each day it continues to heal me of things that has held me back. All praises be unto you forever O Lord is your word settled in heaven. Your truths cannot be broken and never returns to you void. I will not walk like one who just take lives simply because and I will not hate and take my own life committing spiritual suicide.

I shout to the mountain top Jesus I love you more each day for you are a breath of fresh air and you have given me a new hope to love and not hate. To live life to the fullest. Thank you, Father, everyday for your mercy. In Jesus name, Amen

Notes:

_____
_____
_____
_____
_____
_____
_____
_____
_____
_____
_____
_____
_____
_____
_____
_____
_____
_____
_____
_____
_____
_____
_____
_____
_____
_____
_____
_____
_____
_____

Notes:

_____
_____
_____
_____
_____
_____
_____
_____
_____
_____
_____
_____
_____
_____
_____
_____
_____
_____
_____
_____
_____

Day 31 Taking charge

1 Samuel 30:6 And David was greatly distress; for the people spoke of stoning him, because the soul of the people was grieved, every man for his sons and for his daughters: but David encouraged himself in his God.

Glory to God! Have you ever been in a situation where you were in one place to help someone and they just could not trust your true loyalty toward their situation and you were rejected.

Then you get home and the enemy has cause havoc in your home, with your friends, your faithful prayer partners, or church family and they looked at you and pointer at you because of the problem.

That's a hard thing isn't it? You being as broken as they are your family is in trouble too but all they can see is you as the problem and there is absolutely no one around to say let's pray. God will bring you through this, he did it for you before he'll do it again.

This passage of scripture tells us David was in great sorrow his heart was broken not only was the people families taken but all his family was taken from Ziklag as well. 1 Samuel 30:1-5 describes how the women and children were taken, they didn't kill them they took them. So, can you imagine what was going on in these men minds. They wept and lifted their voices until they had no more strength to cry.

But it came to a point for David that he knew I must take charge of me. So, he called for the Ephod and went into prayer to seek God concerning his situation.

When trouble hits us, we must learn to take charge of our lives in prayer to seek God concerning our situation, speak over our situation in the name of Jesus and stop waiting on Bro. and Sis. Bucket mouth to speak an encouraging word in our life.

Today we will take charge and encourage ourselves.

Father we bless you that we are above only and not beneath. We declare today we shall recover all in Jesus name. We declare that we live by the commandments of God.

Our families are strong and mighty in you. Oh, Lord we declare their deliverance from mental and emotional imprisonment.

We declare that the spirit bondage is broken, and generational curses are destroyed. We snatch our peace from the claws of the enemy and every evil word that has gone up against our lives today we take charge through the power of the Holy Ghost and the blood of Jesus and destroy these words. We snatch them down and we reverse negativity with the word of God that says we are overcomers, victorious, fearfully and wonderfully made.

I speak that our children are prosperous. They finish strong in everything they have been called and assigned to do. The weapons that form against them will never prosper for I declare their lives to belong to God, for they are my seed and I am the seed of Christ Jesus.

We declare that everything the enemy thought he would take, my family and friends, neighbors, churches and community we take charge and release the word of God declaring we shall recover all.

We declare this day we are over it, the fear, pain, hurt disappointment and low-self-esteem. We shall encourage ourselves daily knowing that we are the righteousness of God in the Holy name of Jesus Amen.

Notes:

Notes:

Day 32 Watching my words

Psalms 141:1-3

Lord, I cry unto thee: make haste unto me; give ear unto my voice, when I cry unto thee. 2. Let my prayer be set forth before thee as incense; and the lifting of my hands as the evening sacrifice. 3. Set a watch, O Lord, before my mouth; keep the door of my lips.

We should cry out to the Lord daily. If we look at day 32 David prayed to encourage himself and to receive instructions from God. His posture in prayer was different. David asked for the priest Abiathar to bring him the ephod a garment that the priest used to pray for the nations or twelve tribes of Israel but today his hands are lifted.

When we lift our hands unto God it is saying to him I surrender all unto you. When we cry out to the Lord we must be attentive to what we are saying not only that but attentive to what we are saying to others. As we grow stronger in seeking the heart of God we will change our conversation with him.

With this I simply mean instead of always asking him to do it you will trust that it's already done. How can you see the change in your prayer language? Well the words from your mouth begin to speak of you being thankful in advance, you will declare things over your life and others, you will seek his will and not just your desires you may have.

Instead of asking him to do it all the time, you will seek him to see what you must do for him. Pray language major change is when you go to him simply because you love him.

You love on the Lord and let him know how much you value Him for just being God. In your process of deliverance,

you will learn talking with the Father becomes pleasurable because you now understand you have never been alone on this life journey. So, we must always guard our words.
I declare that the Lord has heard my voice and he understands my cry. I Declare my prayers are a sweet smell in the nostrils of the Lord. I Declare I am attentive to the words that proceed from my lips.

My words are strength to others.

My words speak the essences of God's love.

Father in the name of Jesus, thank you for hearing my cry and your ears being open to my voice. I am grateful for you setting a watch before my mouth and giving me temperance over the door of my lips. I will be quickly to hear and slowly to speak and slow to anger.

Even Lord as you patiently attend to hear me so shall I attend to hear others. I will not allow myself to indulge in the wicked works of men's inequities nor sit at their table as they celebrate with self-indulgence. I will take criticism and weigh each word carefully considering to be a kindness that is shown towards me.

I will be wise and keep quiet because you have always been there for me and I trust you. I take charge of my words and I will be positive, leaving negative thoughts, people and words behind me. Hallelujah in Jesus name

Notes:

_____
_____
_____
_____
_____
_____
_____
_____
_____
_____
_____
_____
_____
_____
_____
_____
_____
_____
_____
_____
_____
_____
_____
_____

Notes:

Day 33 Tongue of the Wise

Proverbs 15:1-4 A soft answer turn away wrath: but grievous words stir up anger. 2. The tongue of the wise useth knowledge aright: but the mouth of a fool pours out foolishness. 3. The eyes of the Lord are in every place, beholding the evil and the good. 4. A wholesome tongue is a tree of life: but perverseness therein is a breach in the spirit.

The book of Proverbs are life lessons that Solomon wrote giving godly wisdom and knowledge that we may apply to our lives. Proverbs 15 starts out letting us know if you do not scream, yell, rant and rave people can't hear you and the act of retaliation would come forth.

When responding to someone tone of voice means something. Our words matter the way we present them even when we speak to those that may have wronged us or may be presenting their issues before us. The soft answer the love of God through our speaking can change the complete atmosphere.

I had my moments that I did not have a soft answer for people and instead of peace and problems being solved the problem worsened. Why? Because I acted like a fool rather than a wise child of God. I did not set a watch before my mouth, I let it reap. I wasn't quickly to hear and slowly to speak, I acted out of my emotions rather than the spirit of God.

We all have behave foolishly but now we must renounce the fool's mentality and cling to the wisdom of God. Our words can bring deliverance or war. Chose deliverance and peace today.

We declare we speak with a tender voice bringing forth a soft answer.

We declare our words will not be grievous words to others.

We declare our tongues to be wise and it use knowledge.

We declare our tongues are wholesome and is like the tree of life.

We declare our lips give out knowledge.

Father as we make these declarations over our words we understand that to declare a thing simply says we will walk it out. It is not enough for me to speak it but I must do it. So, I speak over my life today, I will live the life that I speak of daily.

My mouth will exalt and edify your name Lord and you will receive the glory out of my life and all the world will know that you are my King.

Notes:

Notes:

_____
_____
_____
_____
_____
_____
_____
_____
_____
_____
_____
_____
_____
_____
_____
_____
_____
_____
_____
_____
_____
_____
_____
_____
_____

Day 34 The floods have lifted

Psalms 93:1-5 The Lord reign, he is clothed with majesty; the Lord is clothed with strength, wherewith he hath girded himself: the world also is established, that it cannot be moved. 2. Thy throne is established of old: thou art from everlasting. 3 The floods have lifted, O Lord, the floods have lifted their voice; the floods lift their waves. 4. The Lord on high is mightier than the noise of many waters, yea, than the mighty waves of the sea. 5. Thy testimonies are very sure: holiness becometh thine house, O Lord forever.

Our God is complete royalty, he is the epitome of what a true King represents. In fact, he is the only true King, although there be many kings. This division of Psalms speaks of one the Lord reigning holding royal position, being sovereign walking as our royal King his garment is full of beauty and layered with strength.

The world being established by him it was set solid. His throne was before the beginning of time. Everything was created by him and for him we must obey at his command. The house of God is beautified with holiness. Our God is King of all kings and there is none to compare to his majesty. As you pray place your words in the empty spaces let there be strength in my family, this is just an example of what you may want to place in the paces. We are now progressing to a place where you pray and speak over your life and others more freely. These prayers should now be an extension of your prayers.

Remember we are breaking the strongholds that have had us bound.

Notes:

_____
_____
_____
_____
_____
_____
_____
_____
_____
_____
_____
_____
_____
_____
_____
_____
_____
_____
_____
_____
_____
_____
_____
_____
_____

Notes:

Day 35 Setting my affections on Christ

Colossians 3:1-4 If ye then be risen with Christ, seek those things which are above, where Christ sitteth on the right hand of God. 2. Set your affection on things above, not on things on the earth. 3. For ye are dead, and your life is hid with Christ in God. 4. When Christ, who is our life, shall appear, then shall ye also appear with him in glory.

Paul's expression in these passages speaks of what our true behavior should be as sons of God not walking in self- denial for vain purposes but submitting our hearts to God

Changing our way of thinking, walking with greater morals and standards in Christ. Seeking heavenly things more so then the pleasures of this world. Recognizing that we are covered, protected and guarded in God through Christ Jesus.

Even as sons of God we may still struggle in our flesh but Paul in Colossians chapter 3 says to get control of ourselves and do away with the things that cast a shadow of darkness over us. Fear and torment, anger and bitterness cast a shadow over us either a shadow of weightiness or sin.

We who once walked in darkness no longer have to submit to sin for we have buried the old man with Christ and because of him we walk with the newness of God.

As people there are many things that we may go through, broken relationships, loss of jobs, loss of home, friends and love ones. Moments when it appears as though it is one thing after the next but one thing I know, when you allow yourself to be hid in Christ and you set your affections on things of God you can endure things in this world better.

Our hope should never be in the world but in the Creator of the world God our Father the virtuous and Holy one of Israel.

Father we thank you for this moment and time that we have been blessed to share with you. We continually daily submit ourselves unto you. We speak that we have been risen with you and now we seek daily the things in heaven.
We recognize that this life is temporary, and our affections are to be set on your will and desires. We declare that our life is hid with Christ in God. We declare we are guarded, shielded, protected and covered by God.
We speak over our minds and bodies commanding them to obey the spirit of God mortifying the deeds our bodies. We openly resist fleshly lust and walk in the spirit of God in Jesus name. We put old things that have lingered in our lives and cause a stagnation to take place down.
We cast out disobedience, anger, malice, wrath and blasphemy and filthy communication out of our mouths. We are renewed in God and walk as a new person. My mind is stronger, my thoughts are clearer now because of my submitting to God, no longer am I afraid. For I truly am a son of God.
I speak now that every wicked imagination is cast down and burned with Holy Ghost fire. I declare a heavenly hedge to be placed about my life now. I speak every open door to the enemy has now been closed and sealed with the blood of Jesus Christ.

We apply the blood of Jesus over our Spirit, soul and body. The blood of Jesus is against you Satan all power rests in my Father hands.

My Father is Royalty which makes me royal through him. I will keep my mind stayed on him in Jesus name, Amen

Notes:

Notes:

_____
_____
_____
_____
_____
_____
_____
_____
_____
_____
_____
_____
_____
_____
_____
_____
_____
_____
_____
_____
_____
_____
_____
_____
_____

Day 36 At the name of Jesus

Philippians 2:9-11 Wherefore God also hath highly exalted him, and given him a name which is above every name: 10. That at the name of Jesus every knee should bow, of things in heaven and things in earth, and things under the earth; 11. And that every tongue should confess that Jesus Christ is Lord, to the glory of God the Father

There is so much power in the name of Jesus that at his name everything and everyone will bow to his glorious name. Each day you have prayed you have submitted you issues to the Lord, renouncing the power the enemy thought he would hold over your life forever.

Fear is a name weakness is a name and it has to surrender to the name of Jesus. Even when unexpected things crop up in our lives that would try to push us back in a place of fear or weakness remember to call on Jesus and submit the issues because Jesus now sit on the right hand of the Father and the Father has given him great power and authority so much that when we call on his name and we do not have any words other then his name to say that name Jesus begin to intercede on our behalf.

Prayer:

Father in the name of Jesus we thank you for the power you carry for right when I thought I had Conquered everything other issues began to rise before me before the I thinking that because of you I can call on your name in at your name the enemy must bow the enemy of sickness in fear and weakness must bow down to you. I think you lord God For increasing my faith in knowing that when I call upon your name surely you will answer I walk with a greater confidence even though trials yet come my way I now understand that there is power in the name of Jesus I now understand that I do not have to fear I do not have to worry if I trust you for your Father has given you a name that is above all names.

I am strong because of Jesus
I am free from Anxiety

Notes:

Notes:

_____
_____
_____
_____
_____
_____
_____
_____
_____
_____
_____
_____
_____
_____
_____
_____
_____
_____
_____
_____
_____
_____
_____
_____

Day 37 Taking charge of the night

Psalms 4:8 In peace I will lie down and sleep, for you alone O Lord, will keep me safe.
Psalms 3:5 I lay down and slept, yet Ii woke up in safety, for the Lord was watching over me.
Acts 13:11, Exodus 7:10-12

It is the Lord's desire that we have sweet sleep. There are moments we lay down with a troubled spirit not binding the hand of the enemy that comes to steal our peace and joy. As a child of the Lord we must understand the power that God has given us.

It is imperative that we take charge of the night atmosphere counter attacks, the works of the enemy but we must recognize that greater is he the Lord Jesus Christ which is in us then he the works of darkness that is in the world. we serve the almighty, the all-powerful God and as we submit ourselves until the Lord as we recognize that in which, is in the power we can have sweet rest we can have peace at night. Nightmares and night terrors will not overwhelm us for we will be able to apply the blood as we sleep through our dreams.

So now today we take charge of our night atmosphere and we bind up the works of the enemy we declare joy in the night we declare peace in our night and we declare victory in our morning for we serve the righteous God the holy one of Israel.

Father we thank you tonight, Lord God for your grace and mercy and your strength. Thank you for being a keeper shield and buckler. Thank you, Lord God, for your grace and your mercy that prevails over us. Father we magnify your name Jesus right now because you are a great and holy and righteous and loving and kind, you are El Shaddai. Lord we bless your Holy Name tonight.

God, we appreciate you for being who you are. We take authority over the night atmosphere in the mighty name of Jesus. We blind the eyes of every watcher and scanners through the power of the Holy Ghost. Even as Paul blinded the eyes of the sorcerer so do release the word of God in the atmosphere that the eyes of the sorcerer be blinded in the name of Jesus.

We bind up the works of witches and warlocks soothsayers, astrologers, hoodoo and voodoo workers. Lord oh God, oh God we speak a shift in the atmosphere, power of Deliverance come forth. For I seek after the Lord and not the powers of darkness.

Father confound the mind of the enemy tonight that everything they thought to do will be crushed with a mighty hammer of God. Arise Oh God! let the enemies be scattered.

We speak sweet rest and peace of mind tonight in the mighty name of Jesus. We will not fear, we will stand strong in you Lord God. We apply your blood through the power of the Holy Ghost in the mighty name of Jesus be with our friends and our family, Lord God deliver now and set free. We trust your word.

We lay down in your grace Lord God, for we speak that every plan of the enemy has been spoiled. For the angels of protections has been released around us. Your blood covers us, so we thank you that we shall arise in the morning in your grace, full of joy, peace and love in Jesus name, Amen

Notes:

Notes:

Day 38 The Prayer of Hannah

When we study Hannah in first Samuel chapter one we recognize that she had troubles and issues. She was broken being pushed into a place of a different level of prayer that will open a room to be a prophet Samuel because of her trouble in the cause of different issues that she carries. A priest didn't believe that she was praying. At one point they thought she was drinking but she was not drunk.

A woman named Peninnah the other wife of Elkanah which had children, but Hannah womb had been closed. Broken and torn on the inside desiring to birth a child Hannah sought the Lord diligently out of her heart and by doing so, the Lord heard her just as he will here us today.

Hannah womb was opened she conceived and she was able to rejoice, praise God and give our never-failing God glory. God showed his faithfulness and his goodness to her; her son Samuel was born he was dedicated back to the Lord. Hannah's pain and fear pushed her into that place of prayer to seek God's heart. When our backs are against wall we must know how to reach the heart of God that we may birth that special thing he has placed within us. This is a prayer of victory. **1 Samuel 2:1-11**

And Hannah prayed and said, my heart rejoices in the Lord, mine horn is exalted in the Lord: my mouth is enlarged over mine enemies; because I rejoice in thy salvation. 2. There is none holy as the Lord: for there is none beside thee: neither is there any rock like our God. 3. Talk no more so exceeding proudly; let not arrogance come out of your mouth: for the Lord is a God of knowledge, and by him actions are weighed. 4. The bows of the mighty men are broken, and they that stumbled are girded with strength. 5. They that were full have hired out themselves for bread; and they that were hungry ceased: so that the barren hath born seven; and she that hath many children is waxed feeble. 6. The Lord killeth, and maketh alive: he bringeth down to the grave, and bringeth up. 7.

The Lord maketh poor, and maketh rich: he bringeth low, and lifteth up. 8. He raiseth up the poor out of the dust, and lifteth up the beggar from the dunghill, to set them among princes, and to make them inherit the throne of glory: for the pillars of the earth are the Lord's, and he hath set the world upon them. 9. He will keep the feet of his saints, and the wicked shall be silent in darkness; for by strength shall no man prevail.

10. The adversaries of the Lord shall be broken to pieces; out of heaven shall he thunder upon them: the Lord shall judge the ends of the earth; and he shall give strength unto his king and exalt the horn of his anointed.

Notes:

_____

_____

_____

_____

_____

_____

_____

_____

_____

_____

_____

_____

_____

_____

_____

_____

_____

_____

_____

_____

_____

_____

_____

_____

_____

Notes:

_____
_____
_____
_____
_____
_____
_____
_____
_____
_____
_____
_____
_____
_____
_____
_____
_____
_____
_____
_____
_____
_____
_____

Day 39 Wise Words

Ecclesiastes 10:12a The words of a wise man's mouth are gracious.

As we grow and learn the power that we truly possess in God our word must be carefully used. The Lord has called us to be wise in him and our wise to produce wisdom. This day we will make a declaration over our Mouth.

We declare we are wise men and our mouth shall speak gracious words. (kind, pleasant, merciful, compassionate words). We declare our lips will speak that which is acceptable by God. (**Proverbs 10:32a**)

We declare our tongues shall promote good, ethical, clean, pure, innocent and moral well – being. (**Proverbs 15:4a**)

Father we thank you that in this journey our conversation has changed from words of defeat and fear to words of wisdom and strength.

The blessings of the Lord are now overtaking me, and fear is no longer an option in my life but now Father walking in the divine strength of your power is my only option.

I am learning of you everyday and the more I meditate upon your word the more I realize you never left.

Though man tried to slay me you watched over me. I understand that I could have been dead, but death had no power over me because in your appointed time the things that had me bound you showed me how to become free. Through a manifestation of your word, through my mouth, Satan spirit of torment had to flee. I will continue to confess my deliverance, my family and friend's deliverance, for my tongue is as choice silver and with it we shall prosper. Now when men ask me of my faith my, words will be seasoned with truth and grace and I will know how to respond.

I will not be easily offended but I weigh out the words of others and respond as one with the tongue of the learned. In Jesus name, Amen

Notes:

Notes:

Day 40 I will maintain my integrity

Proverbs 11:3 The integrity of the upright shall guide them: but the perverseness of transgressors shall destroy them.

1 Peter 3:16 Having a good conscience; that, whereas they speak evil of you as of evildoers, they may be ashamed that falsely accuse your good conversation in Christ.

Having integrity is a powerful strength and weapon for one to have because to hold fast to their morals and honesty, in and out of the presence of people. They carry strong ethics and they are trustworthy.

We are here in day forty recognizing that our integrity will speak volumes and our battles will always be won even when our position does not look like what God has promised us. In the book of Genesis beginning in chapter 37 throughout chapter 43 it tells the story of Joseph how he was favored by his Father and dealt with hatred from his brothers.

It speaks of him dreaming and see first his brothers bowing before him and in his second dream he saw his father, mother and siblings bow before him but their bitterness towards him had him placed in a pit and then sold.

The promise established in Joseph's dream never showed him being hated are being put in a pit by his brothers. It did not show his brothers stripping him of the coat of many colors that his father made for him. I can only imagine Joseph being placed in a cold muddy hole with no food, or fresh water hearing his brothers conspire against him, the tears and pleading he may have done. Asking what have done to you to be treated like this after all this was their brother.

Although they wanted to kill him Reuben would not allow it. He persuaded them to place Joseph in the pit but while he was gone they sold him to the Ishmaelites for 20 pieces of silver and brought into Egypt and sold to Potiphar an officer of Pharaoh's and a captain of the guard.

Picture in your mind the trauma, being rejected, betrayed, talked about, judged and sentenced to a life of bondage by your family. Oh, the thoughts Joseph must have had to deal with in his mind but, yet he maintained integrity.

Not understanding why, he is now in a strange land being sold a slave but worked faithfully and found favor in the house of Potiphar. He managed the things in Potiphar's house well but even their trouble and false accusation was lurking. Potiphar's wife wanted to sleep with Joseph, but he would not do it he was honest yet again he was lied on.

Now he is sitting in a person cell this isn't what his dream looked like. Sometimes because of the issues we dealt with it made us prisoners in our mind. Look your position may not look like what God promised you but that rejection, false accusation, being hated, abuse all those things were a set up to guide you into your promise.

In the darkest moment of Joseph's life being imprisoned a shield of protection was still there. He had favor with the warden and yet found himself being a leader in prison. He begins to interpret dreams. He interpreted the dreams of the cupbearer and the baker only saying remember me tell about me, Joseph thought favor was there and God kept him, he wanted to be free.

The baker died as Joseph said and the cupbearer went back and served Pharaoh. The butler forgot about Joseph, but God had an appointed time for Joseph to come forth out of prison. (Genesis chapter 41) The butler remembered Joseph had interpreted his dream and he spoke of to Pharaoh of the man that told him of his dreams.

During this time Pharaoh had dreams that troubled him that no one could give him understanding concerning the dream. The Lord had Joseph positioned in place to do so, you see if he had not been in the prison he would not have met the baker and the cupbearer, and his name would not have been hanging in the atmosphere as to being one that could interpret dreams.

Sometimes our greatest pain is to put us in our greatest position for promise. Joseph went through all of this to bring deliverance to his family and others. The end of the story in Joseph's life his pain turns to joy in all that he went through those ugly seemingly unfair positions he realized it was only to fulfill God's promise.

Now as you begin to look over your life rejoice and again I say rejoice things have occurred in your life, some things you never could have imagined but God kept you. Fear is not an option it is time to live, to love again, to walk in hope, and laugh again without the tears pouring on the inside.
I pray this prayer journal has blessed you. Let us pray

Prayer

Father in the name of Jesus we thank you for your goodness and mercy, we thank you Lord God for all that you've done and all that you will continue to do in our lives. There is no doubt that your all-seeing eyes have been looking over us throughout the times in our lives.

We declare that we are strong today stronger than we've ever been.

We declare our integrity will guide us.

We speak over our lives fresh rivers flowing from our belly.

We declare we are fit for the kingdom, for our eyes are on you Lord. Each day as we awaken we with purpose look to the Hills from which cometh our help knowing that all I help come from you. Each day as we move we will depend on you Father to order our steps, we release our thoughts to obtain your thoughts.

We declare we will think upon the things that are true, honest, just, pure and lovely according to Philippians 4:8.

Finally, we declare despite what comes our way we will maintain our integrity in Jesus. For our hope is built on nothing less than Jesus blood and righteousness.

We are free and we will stay free for whom the Son of man set free is free indeed. **John 8:36**

In Jesus name, Amen

Notes:

Notes:

_____
_____
_____
_____
_____
_____
_____
_____
_____
_____
_____
_____
_____
_____
_____
_____
_____
_____
_____
_____
_____
_____
_____
_____

Synopsis

Sherese is married to Chief Apostle Charles Bolar they work closely together in ministry fulfilling the call of God traveling the nations speaking and preaching life, joy and strength back into God's people. Seeking the Lord that people may receive the Holy Ghost and gain the promised power by Jesus Christ.

She and Apostle Bolar go out restoring hope and annihilating the spirit of fear that has consumed many because of life mishaps. She stands firm on family being the first ministry in her life as a wife and mother. Believing if she stands in the first mention of family that she can walk in the righteous order of God.

Sherese Bolar is the founder of Unity Broken But Not Destroyed Outreach Inc. where she has organized classes with women called Real Talk Real Word dealing with life's issues. Through these sessions ladies were able to look at the root of their problems and deal with them accordingly. She has created a food pantry that help families that are destitute, as well as issue out clothing. She believes that God laid out a clear job description for his people (Matthew 25).

Each year they celebrate families during the Thanksgiving and Christmas holiday when sun isn't shining as much and the green grass is now brown the leaves that once blew in the wind is now being raked off the ground, our Fall and winter months; it is during this time that we have discovered the spirit of depression and fear becomes a great issue in the lives of many.

When mothers and fathers may begin to Fear being alone, fear of not being able to provide for their children with the festive meals or the electronics, dolls and games that other children may obtain during this season.

It was through life's amazing experiences, watching children daily come in and out of her class hungry, angry, sometimes afraid, looking and speaking with parents that were depressed, worrying about their what next. This unction

Sherese Bolar to create an outreach when she had to overcome depression, fears, anger, bitterness and strife in her own life. Her issues made it clear to her that she wasn't the only one dealing with problems in life so after God delivered her she wanted to reach out to others. Now she is reaching the world by giving to those in need with the help of wonderful people that share the same vision.

People empowering People. For her Fear is not an option and defeated she will not be. Sherese is also the Assistant Pastor of Unity Full Gospel, she is a certified life coach and taught pre-k for 18 years using the Abekas system the curriculum that teaches children scriptures from a-z.

She worked under her late Mother in the gospel Prophetess Jean L. Moore of Grace Temple Academy and years later for Co-Pastor Cassandra Crum of Life and Salvation and Victorious Kidz Academy she received her Early Childhood Education from Independence Correspondence School and Chattahoochee Technical college. She studied at Millennium Life Center under Dr. Franco Jordan to develop the Prophetic anointing in her life.

She was licensed as Prophetess in 2006 by Chief Apostle Charles Bolar and later confirmed as an Apostle by Apostle Barbara Steward.

34880391R00098

Made in the USA
Columbia, SC
19 November 2018